SOME KIND OF BLACK

SOME KIND OF BLACK

Nymeria Publishing LLC

First published in the United States of America by
Nymeria Publishing LLC, 2021

Copyright © 2021 by Amber Moss

All rights reserved. Except as permitted under the U.S. Copyright Act of 1976, no part of this publication may be reproduced, distributed, or transmitted in any form or by any means, or stored in a database or retrieval system, without the prior written permission of the publisher.

Nymeria Publishing
PO Box 85981
Lexington, SC 29073
Visit our website at www.nymeriapublishing.com

ISBN 978-1-7363027-6-7

Printed in U.S.A

To My Daughter.
May she never forget her heritage.

Some Kind of Black

I don't know how to dance
so I must not really be black.
I guess rhythm flew right past me
and imprinted into someone more black.
Not my words, but the kids from middle school
who labeled me an Oreo.

I must not really be black
since I'm afraid to throw chicken
in a pot full of hot oil leaving
the task to my sister or mother, or anyone
who's around the kitchen.

But I must be some kind of black
my hair tells me as it coils at my scalp
and my nose whispers to my ass
You are black

What kind of black I do not know
since my lips thin at the top
and my tongue speaks quietly.

I birthed a baby girl
with yellow skin and flushed cheeks
and strangers ask me
Is she completely black?

She is as black as I am
which I guess doesn't mean much
but my mother tells me

Thank God she's light-skinned,
her life depends on it.

Resume Name

I wish my mom had named me
Keisha or Latasha
erase my resume name.

I want a name you can't find
on a keychain at Disneyworld
or in a Times Square "I Love NYC" store.

Give me blackness on my tongue
when I speak, delivering culture
and history of West Atlanta.

When you see my mom
tell her I earned a name
you would find in Harriet's diary.

All Grown Up

At thirteen years old
black boys didn't like me.

small breasted girl
all forehead and nose,

high-waters clenching
to my thighs with green veins

lined up like fractions

in the hallways
they would stare

tried to fix me woman myself
fit into puberty like jeans.

we arrived at the cafeteria
and I ate filled my body

with pork fat and carbs
enough to grow an ass

but the black boys still didn't like me.

I watched a kid build a piñata
so the boys could swing

at her candy. Now twenty-six years old
I wear red lipstick in the woods

and erections follow me to log
cabins down the Chattahoochee.

Adolescence

As the sky collided with the trees,
I gripped my belly. Bent over
while a single red dot blended
into cotton sheets. I waited
for the diagram of my uterus
to inflate along with my breasts,
like pupils as soon as night falls
and the sun escapes
with my innocence.

I wondered how long it would be
until I blossomed into beauty;
Wide hips made room
for the blood flow between
my legs, I opened for the boy
in third period; he examined
my newfound body
then left after a few handfuls.

Monarchy

I am a wide-hipped, big nose,
weave-wearing woman
according to most of America.
I settle for the wrong men:
lined-up, straight edge, earring
wearing dark men with pants hanging
below their asses, oversized t-shirts
the same color as their sneakers.

the good ones are all taken

married to ivory skin and green eyes
more exotic and rare than the ebony
and brown across the street.

*Queens don't come from Detroit
or Atlanta...*

Meet them in England or Brazil,
maybe an Irish lady to be your muse
stroke her crimson hair while she strokes
your ego and your manhood even
harder.

To the sovereign in America, raising the same boys
that grow up to alienate the wide-hipped, big nose,
weave-wearing women...

black diamonds are the most difficult to cut.

* *first published in The Black Girl Archives*

Working Class

I was born to work
like my mother and hers
alike. Carry hands that soothe
flesh and bury bags of secrets
underneath the house that desperately
seeks to be made a home.

I Am Just Like My Mother

My mother walks to the kitchen barefoot,
her hair wrapped and smelling of shea butter.
It is always in the morning when I admire her;
Years of unwed life can change a person.
Like how she doesn't cook breakfast for anyone
but herself.
Cook your own food, she says;
and she doesn't style her hair some days
with no one to scold her for it.
She is self-governed and no longer confined
in a man's world.

As I walk through the door with my Jimmy Choo heels,
I realize I am nothing like my mother.
A contoured face and crimson lips stare at her silk gown while she
cooks; grease and eggs sizzle in the pan and I cringe.
My mother never backs away from the skillet.
Specks of cocoa drops on her arms show years of cooking, while my
undisturbed skin says,
amateur.

As my mother sways her hips to the rhythm and blues humming from
the television,
I picture her as a young girl. A dissident in the 70s,
sprawled out on the couch with her shades
blocking out anyone who tries to speak to her.
Red streaks of color running through her hair while my grandmother
strokes it gently as my mother
bobs her head to Michael Jackson.

Lay back and groove with mine, you gotta feel that heat.
My mother's sultry voice fills my head, and I smile as I realize...

I am just like my mother.

* *first published in Bewildering Stories*

The First Time I Saw You Cry

in a car next to the suites in sunshine
state you said, don't remember this
moment when I'm gone. A mother's tears
draped over leather aren't worth
remembering.

Your hand cradling the bag
he bought you before slicing through
years of love rituals.

It's funny how memory works.

You age but your fingers still
quiver when touching something new

find solace in traditions and familiar
destinations across the lake.

In the evening, you pray
knees digging into the shag carpet

It's the only time I see you cry again
when I'm peeking around the corner

hear sorrow bouncing off your tongue.

These days I hear a mother weeping again
spilling from my own mouth.

Summer in The Countryside

In the countryside we danced
barefoot, red clay sniffing at our toenails
five acres of beetles, and ants,
centipedes inhabiting the land
I once called home.

In the middle of the dirt
a small speaker played
The Temptations
until the sky turned orange
and our eyelids inhaled sleep
before the stars took over the heavens.

It was July
when the sun soaked us in sweat
and we nourished the soil
with our fluids.

86,400 minutes
we grew with the land
kicked around orange peels
before the city yanked us
back to materiality.

26% Other

My sister once took
an ancestry DNA test.

74% Sub-Saharan African
and the rest,
British and Irish.

I turn to the mirror and see
my darkened skin and large nose,
a reflection of my father and mother.

I don't recognize the other 26%
that occupies my blood, but I assume
it's the men that plucked my ancestors
from the fields of Nigeria and made them their own.

Imagine not being whole.

Creeping past the dirt of St. Augustine
through the Niagara River to freedom,
but never escaping
the other 26% that boils in your blood.

It makes me uneasy and I blame it on the history
books who tell me that the emancipation proclamation unshackled my ancestors
and pronounced they would be
"forever free"

Until they learn that they are 26% other.

Skin Color as Inconvenience

I don't visit my grandmother enough
13-hour drive to West Atlanta
although I think about it often

guilt-ridden in my slumber as dreams
disclose the last time I've crept up
concrete steps to see her

weathered face and narrowing
eyes concealed by Lens Crafters,
lips of claret that often mistake my name

for my sisters'. I worry sometimes that she'll grow ill
and no one will tell me. Disease ridden immune system eats away at her
nerves while she smiles

swanking about, speaking of luxury fashion
nights at the jazz hall with her posse
kinky knots sweeping across her face.

she is me from another time
promoting counterculture and education

for black women dipped in inconvenience
as we try desperately to gnaw off
all of our brown inches.

I try to remember a day when charcoal
skin was celebrated in America
not a purportless body covered in ash.

Then I see my grandmother
skin immersed in cocoa butter
years of credentials lined along

white walls of her home in a white-washed
gentrified neighborhood once home
to black Americans only.
She feeds my skin sweetened oatmeal

reminds me that blackness can be desirable too.

first published in Liminality Poetry

What Color Is Something Beautiful?

Tell me...

if you could change the color of your skin
would you oblige?

like adding cream to coffee
to sweeten its bitterness,

rip off the bandage of dark cuticles
to expose pastel skin.

How beautiful would I be
with blue eyes,
an unpigmented face?

Would boys crawl under desks
just to swallow my attention?

Sometimes I wake up predawn
and wish to blossom into whiteness

turn my sandaled feet into
bleached cravings.

Tell me...

If you could grasp something beautiful,

what color would it be?

Avoid the Sun

it will leave you darker,
spray bruises on your skin
that resemble vulnerability.

resemble vulnerability and clothe yourself
in long sleeves during torrid weather;
roast by the dirt road.

roast by the dirt road when sweat begins
to dry, no longer masking your skin.

Mask your skin with layers
of SPF, tell your lover
it's for protection.

It's for protection
from the cops and crooks
who make you a target.

Who made you a target?
America.

Stay Alert, Stay Alive

I feed my body kale and salmon

make it strong enough to ward
off the fair skins who claim
my hair is unprofessional.

Dip my limbs into loose jeans,
neutral tops   remain unnoticed on Park Ave
so I don't get tackled or tasered by blue uniforms
on my way to work.

Pray that I don't fit the profile
of the black woman who shoplifted
from the corner store two blocks away.

Walk fast to the office get an alibi
so I don't get killed
accidentally.

There is nothing at the drugstore
to treat black skin

nor do they sell legs fast enough
to help me run from the complexion
my mother birthed me with.

I often think about the words
flashing on interstate signs

Stay alert, Stay alive.

prompting me to stay awake each night.

#1269

When a black man is put on death row
we swallow red, white, and blue tokens
that display the badge of our nation
for justice and peace, celebrating
another brother taken off the streets.
Spread a sheet over a life
promised by our country, innocent until proven
guilty. A reckless night in '89
could lead to wrongful conviction,
a scene of confusion and uncertainty
chasing unreliable witnesses and jailhouse
informants to convict a son.
I don't want a son with dark skin
and nappy hair that I'll have to identify
on a stretcher late at night. How is it
that we have made a culture out of
killing black men or stuffing them
into orange jumpsuits for twenty years?
Sometimes I wish I married a woman
because I fear for my black husband
in this country that prosecutes skin color.

I hope the distance to heaven isn't too far
from the jailhouse.

Loving Black Shadows

No one tells you how hard it is
to love black shadows in America

reach for comfort in a man
whose life is measured by his
height and weight, how intimidating
he looks in a side profile.

Some days I wait for my husband
to get detained, hire lawyers
to prove his innocence while he ages
in a cell waiting for January to bleed
into December until a jury void of
racial composition determines him guilty
of being black.

I tried to curb my appetite

fight back the greedy woman
hungry for a black man's love

let cable convince me
they're all no good.

But how do you regurge a love
that is already built inside of you?

Things My Father Taught Me Part II

1. Black men are warriors. Let them feast on your soul.
2. Today, you are alive; But even the most respected Black woman may die at the hands of a white man.
3. Drag yourself through a Black man's hysteria, and you will still be labeled a Crazy Black Woman.

Black Men Cry Too
(For K.T.)

Last week,
a friend of my dad's
died.

COVID complications
doctor said

as they covered his body
in a sheet as white as
his new Ford truck.

Who will drive it now

to the lot on Eatonton Highway
where Black men sip
Bud Light and talk about
too many gay boys taking over Georgia?

Who gave him the rona?

women scream at my mother

say it was probably the city girl
who keeps coming to the country
for ribs and weed.

words stick to my mother like lip gloss
and she vows to stay away.

On Sunday,
I heard my dad's voice crack
for the first time in nine years

since he found a boy's lips
on my younger sister's breasts.

Back then,
men weren't supposed to cry

especially around small girls who ate
Fruit Loops for breakfast.

Before he started drinking,

my dad wished for heaven
and a God

so K.T. wouldn't feel lonely
in a velvet casket beneath
yards of orange dirt.

I wished for another nine years

to feel salted tears on my shoulder
from the man who taught me
Black men don't cry.

American Soldier

as children we ate water-activated food in a pouch
on cold floors around the tv
a tradition found by two generations of American
soldiers after they've enlisted

our father spit out cadences
while we danced around fruit flies
in the backyard and mother yelled at us
for digging our soles in dirt for her
to scrub off later

in 2003 we grew two years
without our father
held by sunlight while he captured
darkness washed over the desert

I've been told that Black children
live without their fathers all the time
some vanished and some buried

twenty years of service now we eat
around the dinner table
cedar trees tapping at the window
startling my father every so often

Hypothetically, Of Course

Are there some wars not worth fighting?
        -Hypothetically x Lyfe Jennings

Say I have less melanin in my skin,
white-passing as they call it.
Say my hair combs straight
wraps around my neck in the ocean.

Say I get a job interview with Vogue,
Anna Wintour says I dress impeccably.
Say I'm offered the position alongside
executive cultural appropriation and sidelined
token writers.

Let's say you erase black trauma,
lazy stereotyping. Denounce
racial reckoning amidst white superiors.

Say I go to dinner with green hair,
long, acrylic nails, shoes that touch
my thighs and visitors don't gawk
in my presence.

Say we smother the facts
of white privilege in 50 states.
Cover its tracks from Maine
to California. Leave the past behind us.

Hypothetically, of course.

Inspired by Taylor Byas

Say Their Name

I hope you understand
that blackness is precious,
a culture so often available
for profit.

Do not succumb to the disease
of trading your coils for erect strands
to assemble an appearance
of European beauty.

May your voice echo in the streets
of Louisville, Minneapolis, Sanford
without ever being silenced.

Acknowledgements

Thank you to the following literary journals in which some of my work originally appeared in:

Poetry Super Highway

The Black Girl Archives

Bewildering Stories

Liminality Poetry

I would like to express my special thanks to Nymeria Publishing for giving this book a home.

Lastly, I want to thank my husband for reading every poem I wrote and motivating me to keep writing. My darling, you are my inspiration each and every day.

www.ingramcontent.com/pod-product-compliance
Lightning Source LLC
Chambersburg PA
CBHW020916080526
44589CB00011B/616